HUMAN DISCOVERIES AND PROGRESS

The Story of Money Development

Long ago, people hunted or farmed to get their food. Since one person couldn't do everything alone, they traded leftover food and goods with each other. But there were problems: the items were too big and could spoil easily.
So, people agreed to use metals that wouldn't damage as a standard for trade.
Later, they made lightweight and easy-to-store paper money.
Now, it's even more convenient with plastic cards and smartphones for payments.

Self-sufficiency
Make or grow what you need

Bartering
Trading things you need for things you want

Commodity Money
That are easy to store and transport, durable, and scarce as currency.

Minted Currency
Metal is melted down to create a certain weight and shape.

Banknotes
Create and use banknotes that are easy to store and lightweight to carry.

Credit cards, mobile payments
Make it easy to pay for things without carrying cash.

The Story of Democracy Development

In the past, a king made all the decisions.
However, people believed that all humans are equal.
Why should one person hold all the power?
So, they fought for freedom and equality, and eventually, democracy was born.
Now, we can choose our representatives, who manage the country based on our opinions.
We must ensure they keep their promises and watch how they perform their duties.

The Story of Writing Development

Initially, people drew pictures to share their thoughts.
For example, they drew hunting scenes to tell stories about the hunt.
These drawings gradually evolved into an alphabet.
Thanks to the alphabet, reading and writing became much easier.
The invention of paper and printing spread information far and wide, and many people learned to read and write.
With the advent of computers and the internet, we can now easily communicate with people all over the world.

The Story of Science Development

In ancient civilizations, people observed the movements of stars and the changes of seasons to understand the laws of nature.
Ancient philosophers proposed various theories about natural phenomena.
Through the Middle Ages into the Renaissance, scientific methods developed.
They established ways to verify theories through experiments and evidence.
In the 17th and 18th centuries, significant discoveries in physics, chemistry, and biology laid the foundations for various scientific fields.
The Industrial Revolution rapidly advanced technology and science, significantly changing our lives.

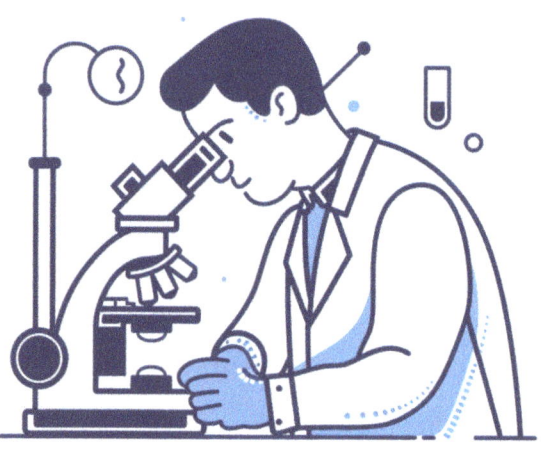

The Story of Economy Development

After understanding the natural world and developing systems of money, democracy, and writing, humans began to think deeply about how economies work. This led to significant discoveries in economic thought.

This journey through economic thought shows how ideas evolve in response to changing economic realities and societal values.

From Smith's advocacy for free markets to Marx's critique of capitalism, Keynes's support for government intervention, and Hayek's defense of the free market, the story of economic development reflects a continuous dialogue on how to improve human welfare through the organization of economic systems.

Adam Smith and 'The Wealth of Nations'

In 1776, Adam Smith, a Scottish economist, wrote "The Wealth of Nations."
He argued that the best economic outcomes come from individuals freely pursuing their own interests.
According to Smith, when people work for their own gain, they unintentionally benefit society by producing what others need.
This concept is known as the 'invisible hand' of the market.

Karl Marx and 'Capital'

In the 19th century, Karl Marx presented a different view in his work, "Capital."

Marx focused on the struggles between classes, specifically between the capitalists, who own the means of production, and the workers, who sell their labor.

He believed that capitalism inherently leads to inequality and would eventually be replaced by socialism and communism, where the workers own the means of production.

John Maynard Keynes

Moving into the 20th century, the Great Depression challenged the ideas of free-market economies.

John Maynard Keynes, in his 1936 book "The General Theory of Employment, Interest and Money," argued that in times of economic downturn, private sector demand may not be enough to achieve full employment.

Keynes suggested that in such times, government intervention through public spending and monetary policies could stimulate demand and pull economies out of recession.

Friedrich Hayek

In contrast to Keynes, Friedrich Hayek, a prominent figure in the Austrian School of economics, emphasized the role of free market and minimal government intervention.

Hayek, in works like "The Road to Serfdom," argued that central planning and excessive government control over the economy lead to a loss of freedom and tyranny.

He believed in the power of the market to organize economic life and allocate resources efficiently.

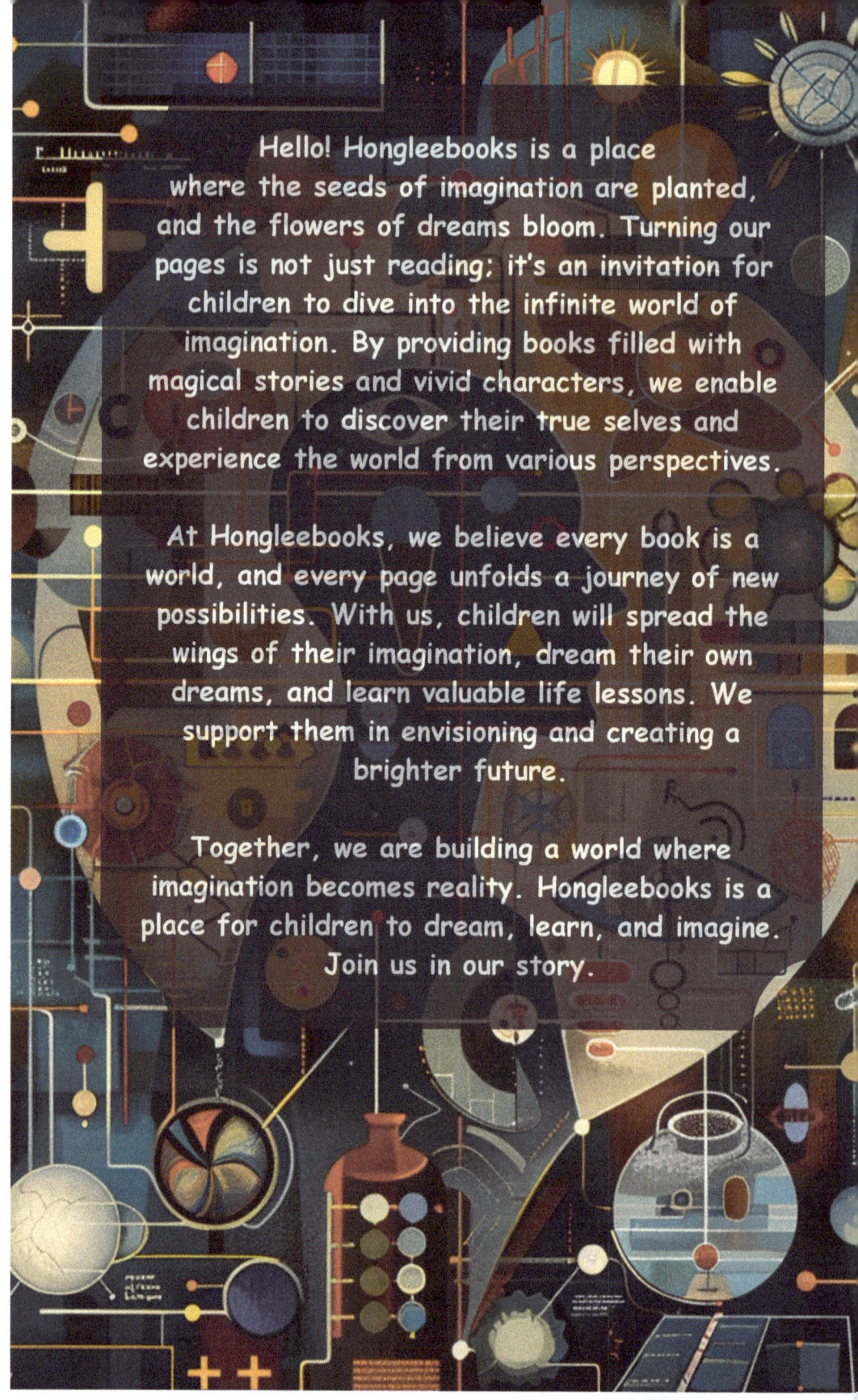

Hello! Hongleebooks is a place where the seeds of imagination are planted, and the flowers of dreams bloom. Turning our pages is not just reading; it's an invitation for children to dive into the infinite world of imagination. By providing books filled with magical stories and vivid characters, we enable children to discover their true selves and experience the world from various perspectives.

At Hongleebooks, we believe every book is a world, and every page unfolds a journey of new possibilities. With us, children will spread the wings of their imagination, dream their own dreams, and learn valuable life lessons. We support them in envisioning and creating a brighter future.

Together, we are building a world where imagination becomes reality. Hongleebooks is a place for children to dream, learn, and imagine. Join us in our story.

www.ingramcontent.com/pod-product-compliance
Lightning Source LLC
LaVergne TN
LVHW051041070526
838201LV00067B/4885